SACRED
SPACE

for Lent 2014

"Inspired by one of the most successful spirituality websites around (and for good reason), *Sacred Space* offers readers short but profound meditations on the daily scriptures. Friendly, concise, and consistently thought provoking, these books are perfect for anyone who would like to pray more and be more connected to God, but may feel too busy to do so. In other words, everyone!"

Rev. James Martin, S.J.
Author of *The Jesuit Guide to (Almost) Everything*

SACRED SPACE

for Lent 2014

from the website www.sacredspace.ie
Prayer from the Irish Jesuits

ave maria press AMP notre dame, indiana

acknowledgment

The publisher would like to thank Brian Grogan, S.J., for his kind assistance in making this book possible. Correspondence with the Sacred Space team can be directed to feedback@sacredspace.ie where comments or suggestions related to the book or to www.sacredspace.ie will always be welcome.

Unless otherwise noted, the Scripture quotations contained herein are from the *New Revised Standard Version* Bible, copyright © 1989 by the Division of Christian Education of the National Council of the Churches of Christ in the United States of America. Used by permission. All rights reserved.

Published under license from Michelle Anderson Publishing Pty Ltd., in Australia.

Founded in 1865, Ave Maria Press is a ministry of the United States Province of Holy Cross.

www.avemariapress.com

Paperback: ISBN-10: 1-59471-437-1, ISBN-13: 978-1-59471-437-5

E-Book: ISBN 10 1-59471-443-6, ISBN-13: 978-1-59471-443-6

Cover design by Andy Wagoner.

Text design by Kristen Hornyak Bonelli.

Printed and bound in the United States of America.

how to use this book

During this Lenten season, we invite you to make a sacred space in your day. Spend ten minutes praying here and now, wherever you are, with the help of a prayer guide and scripture chosen specially for each day. Every place is a sacred space, so you may wish to have this little book available at any time or place during the course of the day—in your desk at work, while traveling, on your bedside table, in your purse or jacket pocket. . . . Remember that God is everywhere, all around us, constantly reaching out to us, even in the most unlikely situations. When we know this, and with a bit of practice, we can pray anywhere.

The following pages will guide you through a session of prayer stages.

Something to think and pray about each
  day this week
The Presence of God
Freedom
Consciousness
The Word (leads you to the daily Lenten
  scripture and provides help with the
  text)
Conversation
Conclusion

It is most important to come back to these
pages each day of the week as they are an integral
part of each day's prayer and lead to the scripture
and inspiration points.

Although written in the first person, the
prayers are for "doing" rather than for reading
out. Each stage is a kind of exercise or medita-
tion aimed at helping you to get in touch with
God and God's presence in your life.

We hope that you will join the many people around the world praying with us in our sacred space.

the presence of God

Bless all who worship you, almighty
God,
from the rising of the sun to its setting:
from your goodness enrich us,
by your love inspire us,
by your Spirit guide us,
by your power protect us,
in your mercy receive us,
now and always.

Something to think and pray about each day this week:

Bringing Light

"Your light will rise in the darkness" (Is 58:10). My life will be a light? My life, my person, who I am? How can that be? Sometimes I look around and see someone whose life is a light; or I remember a person I knew, perhaps a grandparent, who radiated light. Nelson Mandela has been a light, and so too has Gandhi. The movie *Of Gods and Men* portrays a group of Cistercian monks who elect to stay among Algeria's poor, Muslim villagers. Despite mortal threats they decide to do so together, in fear but with consolation in their hearts. They can do no other. In consequence they give their lives. But can I, myself, in my modest circumstances? "If you remove the yoke from among you, the pointing of the finger, the speaking of evil, if you offer your food to the hungry and satisfy the needs of the afflicted, then your light shall rise in the darkness and your gloom be like a noonday" (Is 58:9–10). My hidden life, with my continual effort to be just and upright, to overcome failure, and live with humanity and faith, will be a light. Thankfully, I will not see that myself; yet the light will shine. And Jesus' words will be my guarantee and strength: "You are the light of the world" (Mt 5:14).

The Presence of God

I pause for a moment
and think of the love and the grace that God showers on me,
creating me in his image and likeness, making me his temple.

Freedom

Lord, grant me the grace to be free from the excesses of this life.

Let me not get caught up with the desire for wealth.

Keep my heart and mind free to love and serve you.

Consciousness

In the presence of my loving Creator,
I look honestly at my feelings over the last day,
the highs, the lows, and the level ground.
Can I see where the Lord has been present?

The Word

God speaks to each one of us individually.
I need to listen to what he is saying to me.
(Please turn to your scripture on the following pages. Inspiration points are there should you need them. When you are ready, return here to continue.)

Conversation

Sometimes I wonder what I might say
if I were to meet you in person, Lord.
I might say, "Thank You, Lord" for always
being there for me.
I know with certainty there were times when
you carried me,
when through your strength I got through the
dark times in my life.

Conclusion

Glory be to the Father, and to the Son, and to
the Holy Spirit,
As it was in the beginning, is now and ever
shall be,
World without end. Amen.

Wednesday 5th March,
Ash Wednesday

Matthew 6:1–6

Beware of practicing your piety before others in order to be seen by them; for then you have no reward from your Father in heaven. So whenever you give alms, do not sound a trumpet before you, as the hypocrites do in the synagogues and in the streets, so that they may be praised by others. Truly I tell you, they have received their reward. But when you give alms, do not let your left hand know what your right hand is doing, so that your alms may be done in secret; and your Father who sees in secret will reward you. And whenever you pray, do not be like the hypocrites; for they love to stand and pray in the synagogues and at the street corners, so that they may be seen by others. Truly I tell you, they have received their reward. But whenever you pray, go into your room and shut the door and pray to your Father who is in secret;

and your Father who sees in secret will reward you."

- There may be outward actions I have in mind for this Lent; I invite God to do the inward work on my heart, bringing me to conversion, healing, and growth.

- I pray for the humility I may need to act quietly and discreetly this Lent. How might I experience the conversion God desires for me and learn of my need for God?

Thursday 6th March   Luke 9:23–25

Jesus said to them all, "If any want to become my followers, let them deny themselves and take up their cross daily and follow me. For those who want to save their life will lose it, and those who lose their life for my sake will save it. What does it profit them if they gain the whole world, but lose or forfeit themselves?"

- Lent invites me to consider what I am really looking for as I hear Jesus say that it is possible to gain the world and lose oneself. I ask God to help me, through my time of quiet and prayer, to recognize how I am being called to life.

- There are many ways in which I can enjoy the gains and benefits of the world. How do these distract me from what is for my lasting good? For what wisdom might I ask?

Friday 7th March   **Matthew 9:14–15**

Then the disciples of John came to Jesus, saying, "Why do we and the Pharisees fast often, but your disciples do not fast?" And Jesus said to them, "The wedding guests cannot mourn as long as the bridegroom is with them, can they? The days will come when the bridegroom is taken away from them, and then they will fast."

- The disciples of John compared their religious observation to that of Jesus and his followers.

- Do I sometimes contrast my practice with that of others? Am I drawn either to pride or to despair? Lent calls me to walk humbly with God in company with, and in prayer for, others.

Saturday 8th March   Luke 5:27–32

After this Jesus went out and saw a tax collector named Levi, sitting at the tax booth; and he said to him, "Follow me." And he got up, left everything, and followed him. Then Levi gave a great banquet for him in his house; and there was a large crowd of tax collectors and others sitting at the table with them. The Pharisees and their scribes were complaining to his disciples, saying, "Why do you eat and drink with tax collectors and sinners?" Jesus answered, "Those who are well have no need of a physician, but those who are sick; I have come to call not the righteous but sinners to repentance."

- I need never feel unworthy of being in the presence of Jesus; I can be all the more ready to receive his Word when I know my need. It was for the needy that he came, finding a home among the poor.

- The Pharisees strove to live good lives but went astray when they used those lives as the measure against which to judge everyone else. How judgmental am I if I consider others to have gone astray—as I see it? I pray for compassion and quietly ask God's blessing on those in need.

Something to think and pray about each day this week:

The Gaining of Wisdom

Wisdom is a great yet elusive gift. It may be that I often see, in retrospect, how I was more foolish than wise. I may have been worked up over something, and thought I was in the right, motivated by high ideals. Yet the end result was an unsettling one, leaving me and others more dispirited than at peace. Yet often it is from the failures that wisdom comes. How? When I recover from the attendant blackness and, in a spirit of peace, reflect back on what has happened, I learn something about myself and about life, something I had not seen before or else had not held onto at the crucial time. I gain more self-understanding, the ability to see the wider picture, and the courage to be patient in difficult circumstances. And the openness of my heart to God's presence and teaching leads me along the path of wisdom. "Make me to know your ways, O Lord; teach me your paths. Lead me in your truth, and teach me: for you are the God of my salvation" (Ps 25:4–5). In God's presence, then, let me reflect on life, on what is happening. And in a spirit of blessing and hope, let me go forward, and gain wisdom of heart.

The Presence of God

Jesus waits silent and unseen to come into my heart;
I will respond to his call.
He comes with his infinite power and love.
May I be filled with joy in his presence.

Freedom

I ask for the grace

to let go of my own concerns
and be open to what God is asking of me,
to let myself be guided and formed by my loving Creator.

Consciousness
Knowing that God loves me unconditionally,
I can afford to be honest about how I am.
How has the last day been, and how do I feel now?
I share my feelings openly with the Lord.

The Word
I read the Word of God slowly, a few times over, and I listen to what God is saying to me. (Please turn to your scripture on the following pages. Inspiration points are there should you need them. When you are ready, return here to continue.)

Conversation
Remembering that I am still in God's presence,

I imagine Jesus himself standing or sitting
beside me,
and say whatever is on my mind, whatever is
in my heart,
speaking as one friend to another.

Conclusion

Glory be to the Father, and to the Son, and to
the Holy Spirit,
As it was in the beginning, is now and ever
shall be,
World without end. Amen.

Sunday 9th March,
First Sunday of Lent   Matthew 4:1–10

Then Jesus was led up by the Spirit into the wilderness to be tempted by the devil. He fasted forty days and forty nights, and afterwards he was famished. The tempter came and said to him, "If you are the Son of God, command these stones to become loaves of bread." But he answered, "It is written, 'One does not live by bread alone, but by every word that comes from the mouth of God.'" Then the devil took him to the holy city and placed him on the pinnacle of the temple, saying to him, "If you are the Son of God, throw yourself down; for it is written, 'He will command his angels concerning you,' and 'On their hands they will bear you up, so that you will not dash your foot against a stone.'" Jesus said to him, "Again it is written, 'Do not put the Lord your God to the test.'" Again, the devil took him to a very high mountain and showed him all the kingdoms of the world and their splendor; and he said to him, "All these I will give you, if you will fall down and worship me." Jesus said to him, "Away with you, Satan! For it is written, 'Worship the Lord your God, and serve only him.'"

- In our desire to follow Jesus, there will be temptations, as there were for him. He was tempted to abandon his chosen mission, to use all his power for himself, to trust in himself alone.

- Our temptations may be different, but the reality is the same. Attractions other than the way of Jesus will make demands on us.

- What are some of the temptations I often face? How do I respond to them? Can I ask for strength as I pray today, and each day?

Monday 10th March　　Matthew 25:37–40

The righteous will answer him, 'Lord, when was it that we saw you hungry and gave you food, or thirsty and gave you something to drink? And when was it that we saw you a stranger and welcomed you, or naked and gave you clothing? And when was it that we saw you sick or in prison and visited you?' And the king will answer them, 'Truly I tell you, just as you did it to one of the least of these who are members of my family, you did it to me.'"

- Jesus does not tell this parable to make us afraid but to encourage us in our Christian lives.

- I may not do all these actions, but I pray for those who carry them out in Jesus' name.

Tuesday 11th March　　Matthew 6:7–15

Jesus said, "When you are praying, do not heap up empty phrases as the Gentiles do; for they think that they will be heard because of their many words. Do not be like them, for your Father knows what you need before you ask him. Pray then in this way: Our Father in heaven, hallowed be your name. Your kingdom come. Your will be done, on earth as it is in heaven. Give us this day our daily bread. And forgive us our debts, as we also have forgiven our debtors. And do not bring us to the time of trial, but rescue us from the evil one. For if you forgive others their trespasses, your heavenly Father will also forgive you; but if you do not forgive others, neither will your Father forgive your trespasses."

- I am reminded by Jesus not to let my prayer time become too wordy, I might use a favourite phrase from the Our Father and let it guide me through this day.

- Jesus' prayer brings God into the centre. I am reminded that my prayer is time given to God and is not to be measured by how well I feel afterwards or what insights my mind may have received.

Wednesday 12th March   Luke 11:29–30

When the crowds were increasing, Jesus began to say, "This generation is an evil generation; it asks for a sign, but no sign will be given to it except the sign of Jonah. For just as Jonah became a sign to the people of Nineveh, so the Son of Man will be to this generation."

- Jesus recognized the human tendency to look for results, to seek identifiable signs. God has already blessed me with many signs of grace.

- I take some time to recognize them and ask God's help that I may not miss the messages that may be around me every day.

Thursday 13th March   Matthew 7:7–12

Jesus said to the disciples, "Ask, and it will be given you; search, and you will find; knock, and the door will be opened for you. For everyone who asks receives, and everyone who searches finds, and for everyone who knocks, the door will be opened. Is there anyone among you who, if your child asks for bread, will give a stone? Or if the child asks for a fish, will give a snake? If you then, who are evil, know how to give good gifts to your children, how much more will your Father in heaven give good things to those who ask him! In everything do to others as you would have them do to you; for this is the law and the prophets."

- In the very act of praying we receive something from God. As we open our hearts to God in prayer, his hands are open to give us good gifts. We leave a time of prayer with an increase of faith, hope, and love, which is the consolation of God.

- No time of prayer is wasted; all prayer is in the service of love, and prayer increases within us our capacity to love.

Friday 14th March　　　　**Matthew 5:20–24**

Jesus said to his disciples, "For I tell you, unless your righteousness exceeds that of the scribes and Pharisees, you will never enter the kingdom of heaven. You have heard that it was said to those of ancient times, 'You shall not murder'; and 'whoever murders shall be liable to judgment.' But I say to you that if you are angry with a brother or sister, you will be liable to judgment; and if you insult a brother or sister, you will be liable to the council; and if you say, 'You fool,' you will be liable to the hell of fire. So when you are offering your gift at the altar, if you remember that your brother or sister has something against you, leave your gift there before the altar and go; first be reconciled to your brother or sister, and then come and offer your gift."

- Jesus, you point me from the killing to the hatred behind it, from the deed to the heart that prompts it.

- Show me my heart, Lord, and the corners where I harbor resentment or contempt. Then help me to clean them out.

Saturday 15th March   Matthew 5:43–48

Jesus said to the disciples, "You have heard that it was said, 'You shall love your neighbor and hate your enemy.' But I say to you, love your enemies and pray for those who persecute you, so that you may be children of your Father in heaven; for he makes his sun rise on the evil and on the good, and sends rain on the righteous and on the unrighteous. For if you love those who love you, what reward do you have? Do not even the tax collectors do the same? And if you greet only your brothers and sisters, what more are you doing than others? Do not even the Gentiles do the same? Be perfect, therefore, as your heavenly Father is perfect."

- Words of love and tolerance to our enemies and to all who hurt us are difficult. Jesus has died for all; in our place at the death of Jesus we meet all for whom he died. God knows also that we only slowly bring deep hurts to light. God is lovingly with us in the hurts and in the enmities of our lives.

Something to think and pray about each day this week:

Perfection, in God's Way

Some things put forward in scripture, as ideals for us, seem utterly impossible to attain. "Be holy, for I, the Lord your God am holy" (Lv 19:2). "Be perfect, therefore, as your heavenly Father is perfect" (Mt 5:48). Perfection, utter holiness. And Jesus' words about loving our enemies, and praying for them (Mt 5:44) also seem beyond our reach. Yet, we must learn a way of understanding the highest ideals of scripture. So, for instance, when Jesus says, "If anyone strikes you on the right cheek, turn the other also" (Mt 5:39), it must be related to the time when Jesus himself was struck on the cheek and his own response was, "If I have spoken wrongly, testify to the wrong. But if I have spoken rightly, why do you strike me?" (Jn 18:23). We reach the holiness of loving, and the perfection of being utterly upright, only in God's way, and in God's time. We reach it while still being frail and failing. And, in fact, we do not reach that ideal at all. Rather, it is something done in us, by God's doing and blessing. Lord, sow in the depths of my being your goodness and holiness, and in the ways you know best. Let me rely on you, and not on my own efforts. Let me be in your hands, and trust you, in childlike faith.

The Presence of God

For a few moments, I think of God's veiled presence in things:
in the elements, giving them existence;
in plants, giving them life; in animals, giving them sensation;
and finally, in me, giving me all this and more,

making me a temple, a dwelling-place of the Spirit.

Freedom

God is not foreign to my freedom.
Instead, the Spirit breathes life into my most intimate desires,
gently nudging me towards all that is good.
I ask for the grace to let myself be enfolded by the Spirit.

Consciousness

Knowing that God loves me unconditionally,
I can afford to be honest about how I am.
How has the last day been, and how do I feel now?
I share my feelings openly with the Lord.

The Word

The Word of God comes down to us through the scriptures. May the Holy Spirit enlighten my mind and my heart to respond to the gospel teachings. (Please turn to your scripture on the following pages. Inspiration points are there should you need them. When you are ready, return here to continue.)

Conversation

How has God's Word moved me? Has it left me cold?

Has it consoled me or moved me to act in a new way?

I imagine Jesus standing or sitting beside me, I turn and share my feelings with him.

Conclusion

Glory be to the Father, and to the Son, and to the Holy Spirit,

As it was in the beginning, is now and ever shall be,

World without end. Amen.

Sunday 16th March,
Second Sunday of Lent   Matthew 17:1–9

Six days later, Jesus took with him Peter and James and his brother John and led them up a high mountain, by themselves. And he was transfigured before them, and his face shone like the sun, and his clothes became dazzling white. Suddenly there appeared to them Moses and Elijah, talking with him. Then Peter said to Jesus, "Lord, it is good for us to be here; if you wish, I will make three dwellings here, one for you, one for Moses, and one for Elijah." While he was still speaking, suddenly a bright cloud overshadowed them, and from the cloud a voice said, "This is my Son, the Beloved; with him I am well pleased; listen to him!" When the disciples heard this, they fell to the ground and were overcome by fear. But Jesus came and touched them, saying, "Get up and do not be afraid." And when they looked up, they saw no one except Jesus himself alone. As they were coming down the mountain, Jesus ordered them, "Tell no one about the vision until after the Son of Man has been raised from the dead."

- Transfiguration is about Jesus and about us. When we are with him, we are with the divine. When he is with us, he is with the human. His love, grace, sacraments, peace, and compassion can transfigure us.

- May we be present in prayer to light and brightness, allow light to invade us, and know that the light of Jesus given in baptism is never extinguished.

Monday 17th March,
St. Patrick   Luke 10:1–6

After this the Lord appointed seventy others and sent them on ahead of him in pairs to every town and place where he himself intended to go. He said to them, "The harvest is plentiful, but the laborers are few; therefore ask the Lord of the harvest to send out laborers into his harvest. Go on your way. See, I am sending you out like lambs into the midst of wolves. Carry no purse, no bag, no sandals; and greet no one on the road. Whatever house you enter, first say, 'Peace to this house!' And if anyone is there who shares in peace, your peace will rest on that person; but if not, it will return to you."

- Jesus sent the disciples out to be joyful presences in a troubled world. I am sent in the same way.

- The disciples were sent in a spirit of trust; they were to learn to rely on Jesus and not be distracted. I pray that I may be able to keep my focus and to trust in the presence of God's Spirit as I am sent out on the mission of peace.

Tuesday 18th March　　　**Matthew 23:1–12**

Then Jesus said to the crowds and to his disciples, "The scribes and the Pharisees sit on Moses' seat; therefore, do whatever they teach you and follow it; but do not do as they do, for they do not practice what they teach. They tie up heavy burdens, hard to bear, and lay them on the shoulders of others; but they themselves are unwilling to lift a finger to move them. They do all their deeds to be seen by others; for they make their phylacteries broad and their fringes long. They love to have the place of honor at banquets and the best seats in the synagogues, and to be greeted with respect in the marketplaces, and to have people call them rabbi. But you are not to be called rabbi, for you have one teacher, and you are all students. And call no one your father on earth, for you have one Father—the one in heaven. Nor are you to be called instructors, for you have one instructor, the Messiah. The greatest among you will be your servant. All who exalt themselves will be humbled, and all who humble themselves will be exalted."

- Jesus cautions the disciples against an easy rejection of the Pharisees; you are not to reject them outright but are to be discerning and wise. I ask God to help me to resist any fundamentalist rejection of others and to help me to appreciate good wherever I find it.

- There may seem to be a contradiction between obedience and independence. I pray that I may have the humility to imitate, to receive instruction, and to follow even as I accept the dignity that God gives me by speaking in love directly to my heart.

Wednesday 19th March,
St. Joseph   Matthew 1:18–25

Now the birth of Jesus the Messiah took place in this way. When his mother Mary had been engaged to Joseph, but before they lived together, she was found to be with child from the Holy Spirit. Her husband Joseph, being a righteous man and unwilling to expose her to public disgrace, planned to dismiss her quietly. But just when he had resolved to do this, an angel of the Lord appeared to him in a dream and said, "Joseph, son of David, do not be afraid to take Mary as your wife, for the child conceived in her is from the Holy Spirit. She will bear a son, and you are to name him Jesus, for he will save his people from their sins." All this took place to fulfill what had been spoken by the Lord through the prophet: "Look, the virgin shall conceive and bear a son, and they shall name him Emmanuel," which means, "God is with us." When Joseph awoke from sleep, he did as the angel of the Lord commanded him; he took her as his wife, but had no marital relations with her until she had borne a son; and he named him Jesus.

- Joseph showed discretion even though he might well have felt wronged. I think of how he waited, considering what God had to say before he acted.

- I pray for the restraint I need when I am tempted to act impulsively.

Thursday 20th March   Luke 16:19–31

Jesus said to the Pharisees, "There was a rich man who was dressed in purple and fine linen and who feasted sumptuously every day. And at his gate lay a poor man named Lazarus, covered with sores, who longed to satisfy his hunger with what fell from the rich man's table; even the dogs would come and lick his sores. The poor man died and was carried away by the angels to be with Abraham. The rich man also died and was buried. In Hades, where he was being tormented, he looked up and saw Abraham far away with Lazarus by his side. He called out, 'Father Abraham, have mercy on me, and send Lazarus to dip the tip of his finger in water and cool my tongue; for I am in agony in these flames.' But Abraham said, 'Child, remember that during your lifetime you received your good things, and Lazarus in like manner evil things; but now he is comforted here, and you are in agony. Besides all this, between you and us a great chasm has been fixed, so that those who might want to pass from here to you cannot do so, and no one can cross from there to us.' He said, 'Then, father, I beg you to send him to my father's house—for I have five brothers—that he may warn them, so that they will not also come into this place of torment.'

Abraham replied, 'They have Moses and the prophets; they should listen to them.' He said, 'No, father Abraham; but if someone goes to them from the dead, they will repent.' He said to him, 'If they do not listen to Moses and the prophets, neither will they be convinced even if someone rises from the dead.'"

• The rich man had some feeling for his brothers, if little for the poor man at his gate. I pray that my sense of fellowship be broader than any limits of class, country, or religion that the world teaches me to observe.

• God's message is abundantly clear, Jesus says. I ask God to help me to perceive, attend, and follow his Word in this day.

Friday 21st March   **Matthew 21:33–43**

Jesus said, "Listen to another parable. There was a landowner who planted a vineyard, put a fence around it, dug a wine press in it, and built a watch-tower. Then he leased it to tenants and went to another country. When the harvest time had come, he sent his slaves to the tenants to collect his produce. But the tenants seized his slaves and beat one, killed another, and stoned another. Again he sent other slaves, more than the first; and they treated them in the same way. Finally he sent his son to them, saying, 'They will respect my son.' But when the tenants saw the son, they said to themselves, 'This is the heir; come, let us kill him and get his inheritance.' So they seized him, threw him out of the vineyard, and killed him. Now when the owner of the vineyard comes, what will he do to those tenants?" They said to him, "He will put those wretches to a miserable death, and lease the vineyard to other tenants who will give him the produce at the harvest time." Jesus said to them, "Have you never read in the scriptures: 'The stone that the builders rejected has become the cornerstone; this was the Lord's doing, and it is amazing in our eyes.' Therefore I tell you, the kingdom of God will be taken away from you and given to a people that produces the fruits of the kingdom."

- In prayer we often see things in a new way. Like the rejected stone which becomes the central or corner stone, some of our weaknesses and sins can be stepping stones to fuller and deeper life.

- There is a side to prayer which of itself strengthens and heals us; we know that nothing of the worst of life need be final. The Lord can turn weakness into compassion for others, and can bring us through darkness into light. God heals the broken-hearted.

Saturday 22nd March   Luke 15:25–32

Now his elder son was in the field; and when he came and approached the house, he heard music and dancing. He called one of the slaves and asked what was going on. He replied, "Your brother has come, and your father has killed the fatted calf, because he has got him back safe and sound." Then he became angry and refused to go in. His father came out and began to plead with him. But he answered his father, "Listen! For all these years I have been working like a slave for you, and I have never disobeyed your command; yet you have never given me even a young goat so that I might celebrate with my friends. But when this son of yours came back, who has devoured your property with prostitutes, you killed the fatted calf for him!" Then the father said to him, "Son, you are always with me, and all that is mine is yours. But we had to celebrate and rejoice, because this brother of yours was dead and has come to life; he was lost and has been found."

- Maybe the older son reminds me of people I know who are distracted from what is good by judging others things better; I know that I am like this sometimes. I ask God to help me to appreciate my relationships and the gifts I have been given.

- The older son had fallen out of familiarity with the ways of his father; he served him faithfully but did not know his heart. God invites me to keep my prayer time as a time when we converse heart to heart, growing in love and knowledge of one another.

Something to think and pray about each day this week:

Seeing into the Heart

"What is essential is invisible to the eye," says the fox in *The Little Prince* by Antoine de Saint-Exupéry. Yes indeed. But many things in modern life may lead us to rely on outward appearances. Those appearances may satisfy for a while, but there is in fact a deeper seeing, where what is invisible to the ordinary eye will be noticed. For instance, the prophet Samuel heard the words, "The Lord does not see as mortals see; they look on the outward appearance, but the Lord looks on the heart" (1 Sm 16:7). Perhaps a project this Lent might be to cultivate a way of seeing which is deeper than normal. It is a way of seeing that involves my own heart—where I do not rely on outward appearances, but can look inwardly, into myself, and into others. "You desire truth in the inward being; therefore teach me wisdom in my secret heart" (Ps 51:6). Then I can see more clearly into life, and with something of the eyes and wisdom of God. Lord, clear away my blindness, heal me and free me, and let me see clearly.

The Presence of God

Dear Jesus, today I call on you in a special way.
Mostly I come asking for favors.
Today I'd like just to be in your presence.
Let my heart respond to your Love.

Freedom

"I am free."
When I look at these written words
They seem to create in me a feeling of awe.
Yes, a wonderful feeling of freedom.
Thank You, God.

Consciousness

Lord, you gave me the night to rest in sleep.
In my waking hours may I not forget your
goodness to me.
Guide me to share your blessings with others.

The Word

I read the Word of God slowly, a few times
over, and I listen to what God is saying to me.
(Please turn to your scripture on the following
pages. Inspiration points are there should you
need them. When you are ready, return here to
continue.)

Conversation

Dear Jesus, I can open up my heart to you.
I can tell you everything that troubles me.
I know you care about all the concerns in my
life.
Teach me to live in the knowledge
that you who care for me today,

will care for me tomorrow and all the days of my life.

Conclusion

Glory be to the Father, and to the Son, and to the Holy Spirit,
As it was in the beginning, is now and ever shall be,
World without end. Amen.

Sunday 23rd March,
Third Sunday of Lent   John 4:5–10

Jesus came to a Samaritan city called Sychar, near the plot of ground that Jacob had given to his son Joseph. Jacob's well was there, and Jesus, tired out by his journey, was sitting by the well. It was about noon. A Samaritan woman came to draw water, and Jesus said to her, "Give me a drink." (His disciples had gone to the city to buy food.) The Samaritan woman said to him, "How is it that you, a Jew, ask a drink of me, a woman of Samaria?" (Jews do not share things in common with Samaritans.) Jesus answered her, "If you knew the gift of God, and who it is that is saying to you, 'Give me a drink', you would have asked him, and he would have given you living water."

- The Samaritan woman might have been angry or fled from this man who broke all the "rules" by speaking to her. Instead, she was astonished—and answered Jesus with a question of her own.

- She may not yet have come to belief, but by her response she laid herself open to something new, which might change her life.

- Am I open to such a confronting, personal encounter with Jesus?

Monday 24th March   Luke 4:24–30

And he said, "Truly I tell you, no prophet is accepted in the prophet's hometown. But the truth is, there were many widows in Israel in the time of Elijah, when the heaven was shut up three years and six months, and there was a severe famine over all the land; yet Elijah was sent to none of them except to a widow at Zarephath in Sidon. There were also many lepers in Israel in the time of the prophet Elisha, and none of them was cleansed except Naaman the Syrian." When they heard this, all in the synagogue were filled with rage. They got up, drove him out of the town, and led him to the brow of the hill on which their town was built, so that they might hurl him off the cliff. But he passed through the midst of them and went on his way.

- The people who listened to Jesus' message were able to accept it only if it did not reflect badly on them. I allow myself to hear any message from God that calls me to growth. I accept that I am on a journey and have not arrived yet.

- Jesus' hearers did not seem to like the reminder of the importance of other nations; perhaps they had grown to think themselves superior. I ask God to help me to correct any false notions I have about myself or about my people.

Tuesday 25th March,
Annunciation of the Lord   Luke 1:26–33

In the sixth month the angel Gabriel was sent by God to a town in Galilee called Nazareth, to a virgin whose name was Mary. And he came to her and said, "Greetings, favored one! The Lord is with you." But she was much perplexed by his words and pondered what sort of greeting this might be. The angel said to her, "Do not be afraid, Mary, for you have found favor with God. And now, you will conceive in your womb and bear a son, and you will name him Jesus. He will be great, and will be called the Son of the Most High, and the Lord God will give to him the throne of his ancestor David. He will reign over the house of Jacob forever, and of his kingdom there will be no end."

• Mary was "much perplexed" by the words of the angel. Her inspiration points were her trust and her faith. She had to rely on her experience of the working of God as she pondered this new direction in her life.

- I hear the Word of God addressed to me: "Do not be afraid, you have found favor with God." I remain alert to any habit of hearing that robs this message of its power.

Wednesday 26th March   Matthew 5:17–19

Jesus said to his disciples, "Do not think that I have come to abolish the law or the prophets; I have come not to abolish but to fulfill. For truly I tell you, until heaven and earth pass away, not one letter, not one stroke of a letter, will pass from the law until all is accomplished. Therefore, whoever breaks one of the least of these commandments, and teaches others to do the same, will be called least in the kingdom of heaven; but whoever does them and teaches them will be called great in the kingdom of heaven."

- Jesus saw the continuity of God's message; he spoke as had the prophets of old. I realize that I too have a history and tradition.

- I ask God to continue to bless me and to lead me into the wisdom that Jesus had. I pray in respect for all who teach the faith that has come to us from the apostles.

Thursday 27th March   Luke 11:14–20

Jesus was casting out a demon that was mute; when the demon had gone out, the one who had been mute spoke, and the crowds were amazed. But some of them said, "He casts out demons by Beelzebul, the ruler of the demons." Others, to test him, kept demanding from him a sign from heaven. But he knew what they were thinking and said to them, "Every kingdom divided against itself becomes a desert, and house falls on house. If Satan also is divided against himself, how will his kingdom stand?—for you say that I cast out the demons by Beelzebul. Now if I cast out the demons by Beelzebul, by whom do your exorcists cast them out? Therefore they will be your judges. But if it is by the finger of God that I cast out the demons, then the kingdom of God has come to you."

- Even the best of actions are open to misjudgment. I pray that I may seek out the best interpretation of the events around me and ask for the inspiration of God's spirit as I do.

- Where I notice good, I give thanks to God who is at work in the world. In thought, I gather what is good and life-giving now and offer thanks to God.

Friday 28th March Mark 12:28–34

O ne of the scribes came near and heard them disputing with one another, and seeing that he answered them well, he asked him, "Which commandment is the first of all?" Jesus answered, "The first is, 'Hear, O Israel: the Lord our God, the Lord is one; you shall love the Lord your God with all your heart, and with all your soul, and with all your mind, and with all your strength.' The second is this, 'You shall love your neighbor as yourself.' There is no other commandment greater than these." Then the scribe said to him, "You are right, Teacher; you have truly said that 'he is one, and besides him there is no other'; and 'to love him with all the heart, and with all the understanding, and with all the strength,' and 'to love one's neighbor as oneself'—this is much more important than all whole burnt offerings and sacrifices." When Jesus saw that he answered wisely, he said to him, "You are not far from the kingdom of God." After that no one dared to ask him any question.

- The text "Hear, O Israel" would have been one that Jesus learned to pray from an early age. I might count it among the prayers that I know by heart and return to it from time to time, asking God to help me to use all my energies—heart, soul, mind, and strength—in God's service.

Saturday 29th March   Luke 18:9–14

Jesus also told this parable to some who trusted in themselves that they were righteous and regarded others with contempt: "Two men went up to the temple to pray, one a Pharisee and the other a tax collector. The Pharisee, standing by himself, was praying thus, 'God, I thank you that I am not like other people: thieves, rogues, adulterers, or even like this tax collector. I fast twice a week; I give a tenth of all my income.'

But the tax collector, standing far off, would not even look up to heaven, but was beating his breast and saying, 'God, be merciful to me, a sinner!' I tell you, this man went down to his home justified rather than the other; for all who exalt themselves will be humbled, but all who humble themselves will be exalted."

- I place myself with the humble tax collector, asking God for mercy as I realize that I am a sinner. I ask God to help me to know my needs without becoming disheartened.

- The Pharisee did not just think well of himself, but did so at the expense of other people, looking down on them from the height to which he had exalted himself. Are there ways in which I promote myself?

march 30–april 5

Something to think and pray about each day this week:

Open to Mystery

The psalms are wonderful poems and songs for prayer. We can, of course, use our own words, or even simply go beyond words into a silence, a communion beyond what can be spoken. Yet often a phrase from a psalm can catch our mood, or sum up all that our own words are trying to utter. So it is, following from last week's words, "For God alone my soul waits in silence" (Ps 62:1), we might find it helpful to say over and over: "In you, O Lord, I seek refuge; do not let me ever be put to shame; in your righteousness deliver me. Incline your ear to me; rescue me speedily" (Ps 31:1–2). We need that protection always, that lifting up which comes from God. It is true, we need it in human and tangible forms too—from a friend, a person who cares, a spouse, a neighbor. And we in turn offer it to others too. But the source of it all is God. How good, then, when we turn in the depths of our hearts, in the quiet of our being, to prayer before the mystery of God. Especially, if we feel bound, imprisoned in some way, we can reach out to the God who saves: "In your justice, set me free, hear me, and speedily rescue me."

The Presence of God

I pause for a moment
and think of the love and the grace that God showers on me,
creating me in his image and likeness, making me his temple.

Freedom

Everything has the potential to draw forth
from me a fuller love and life.
Yet my desires are often fixed, caught, on illusions of fulfillment.
I ask that God, through my freedom, may
orchestrate
my desires in a vibrant, loving melody rich in
harmony.

Consciousness

In the presence of my loving Creator,
I look honestly at my feelings over the last day,
the highs, the lows, and the level ground.
Can I see where the Lord has been present?

The Word

God speaks to each one of us individually.
I need to listen to what he is saying to me.
(Please turn to your scripture on the following
pages. Inspiration points are there should you

need them. When you are ready, return here to continue.)

Conversation

What feelings are rising in me
as I pray and reflect on God's Word?
I imagine Jesus himself sitting or standing beside me,
and open my heart to him.

Conclusion

Glory be to the Father, and to the Son, and to the Holy Spirit,
As it was in the beginning, is now and ever shall be,
World without end. Amen.

Sunday 30th March,
Fourth Sunday of Lent John 9:1, 6–9, 13–17

As Jesus walked along, he saw a man blind from birth. He spat on the ground and made mud with the saliva and spread the mud on the man's eyes, saying to him, "Go, wash in the pool of Siloam" (which means Sent). Then he went and washed and came back able to see. The neighbors and those who had seen him before as a beggar began to ask, "Is this not the man who used to sit and beg?" Some were saying, "It is he." Others were saying, "No, but it is someone like him." He kept saying, "I am the man." They brought to the Pharisees the man who had formerly been blind. Now it was a Sabbath day when Jesus made the mud and opened his eyes. Then the Pharisees also began to ask him how he had received his sight. He said to them, "He put mud on my eyes. Then I washed, and now I see." Some of the Pharisees said, "This man is not from God, for he does not observe the Sabbath." But others said, "How can a man who is a sinner perform such signs?" And they were divided. So they said again to the blind man, "What do you say about him? It was your eyes he opened." He said, "He is a prophet."

- Jesus' miracles cost him his life because he was claiming to be one with God. The leaders—religious, political—only wanted a savior on their terms.

- After many a healing he disappeared, to get out of sight. Maybe we can do the same: allow ourselves time for faith to grow, to be grateful for our spirituality, and be joyful that we can do something good in the love of our lives for others.

Monday 31st March   John 4:46–50

Now there was a royal official whose son lay ill in Capernaum. When he heard that Jesus had come from Judea to Galilee, he went and begged him to come down and heal his son, for he was at the point of death. Then Jesus said to him, "Unless you see signs and wonders you will not believe." The official said to him, "Sir, come down before my little boy dies." Jesus said to him, "Go; your son will live." The man believed the word that Jesus spoke to him and started on his way.

- The request that the official made of Jesus was simple and direct. I try to be just as I express my desire in prayer.

- The man went on his way confident that Jesus would do as he said. I ask God's help to face the next day with confidence and trust in the Word of God given to me.

Tuesday 1st April John 5:2–9

Now in Jerusalem by the Sheep Gate there is a pool, called in Hebrew Beth-zatha, which has five porticoes. In these lay many invalids—blind, lame, and paralyzed. One man was there who had been ill for thirty-eight years. When Jesus saw him lying there and knew that he had been there a long time, he said to him, "Do you want to be made well?" The sick man answered him, "Sir, I have no one to put me into the pool when the water is stirred up; and while I am making my way, someone else steps down ahead of me." Jesus said to him, "Stand up, take your mat and walk." At once the man was made well, and he took up his mat and began to walk.

- It was evident to Jesus that the man had been beside the pool for a long time; he must have looked as if he was settled in, familiar with the place. As Jesus looks at me, he may see that I am comfortable—even in the limits about which I complain. Do I have the courage to ask Jesus to heal me?

- I pray with compassion for all who believe themselves to be incurable or irredeemable.

Wednesday 2nd April   **John 5:17–23**

Jesus said to the Jews, "My Father is still working, and I also am working." For this reason the Jews were seeking all the more to kill him, because he was not only breaking the Sabbath, but was also calling God his own Father, thereby making himself equal to God. Jesus said to them, "Very truly, I tell you, the Son can do nothing on his own, but only what he sees the Father doing; for whatever the Father does, the Son does likewise. The Father loves the Son and shows him all that he himself is doing; and he will show him greater works than these, so that you will be astonished. Indeed, just as the Father raises the dead and gives them life, so also the Son gives life to whomsoever he wishes. The Father judges no one but has given all judgment to the Son, so that all may honor the Son just as they honor the Father. Anyone who does not honor the Son does not honor the Father who sent him."

- Jesus' relationship to God was threatening to those who saw God differently. He spoke of God as a loving father with whom he related closely, confidently. I think of the relationships that have helped me to understand what Jesus meant. I relax in the presence of God, who loves me deeply.

- Such was the unity of the Father and Jesus that the work of one was the work of the other. Jesus trusts me enough to call me into the same closeness. He reminds me that whatever I do, I do with him, and that what I do to others, I do to him.

Thursday 3rd April   John 5:39–47

Jesus said to the Jews, "You search the scriptures because you think that in them you have eternal life; and it is they that testify on my behalf. Yet you refuse to come to me to have life.

I do not accept glory from human beings. But I know that you do not have the love of God in you. I have come in my Father's name, and you do not accept me; if another comes in his own name, you will accept him. How can you believe when you accept glory from one another and do not seek the glory that comes from the one who alone is God? Do not think that I will accuse you before the Father; your accuser is Moses, on whom you have set your hope. If you believed Moses, you would believe me, for he wrote about me. But if you do not believe what he wrote, how will you believe what I say?"

- Our churches rely on structures, on theology, liturgy, and human organization. Jesus puts all of these in perspective by reminding us of our need to come to him for life; only when we do this will our structures have meaning.

- Jesus placed little value on human acclaim. Do I seek the approval of others too much, forgetting where my true value lies?

Friday 4th April   John 7:1–2, 10, 25–30

Jesus went about in Galilee. He did not wish to go about in Judea because the Jews were looking for an opportunity to kill him. Now the Jewish festival of Booths was near. But after his brothers had gone to the festival, then he also went, not publicly but as it were in secret. Now some of the people of Jerusalem were saying, "Is not this the man whom they are trying to kill? And here he is, speaking openly, but they say nothing to him! Can it be that the authorities really know that this is the Messiah? Yet we know where this man is from; but when the Messiah comes, no one will know where he is from." Then Jesus cried out as he was teaching in the temple, "You know me, and you know where I am from. I have not come on my own. But the one who sent me is true, and you do not know him. I know him, because I am from him, and he sent me." Then they tried to arrest him, but no one laid hands on him, because his hour had not yet come.

- The arguments go to and fro about Jesus: some say that they know nothing about him, others that they know everything. It sometimes seems like that nowadays too, that there are experts on every side.

- I realize that Lent calls me not to be convinced in my mind, but to accept Jesus in my heart. This is the kind of knowledge that Jesus values.

- No matter how much I know about somebody, there always remains much of which is hidden and known only to God. I pray for a deeper reverence of those around me—especially for those I think I know well.

Saturday 5th April   **John 7:50–53**

Nicodemus, who had gone to Jesus before, and who was one of them, asked, "Our law does not judge people without first giving them a hearing to find out what they are doing, does it?" They replied, "Surely you are not also from Galilee, are you? Search and you will see that no prophet is to arise from Galilee." Then each of them went home.

- Nicodemus is an honest man, ready to speak up for truth. I ask God for courage to speak for truth, even at the risk of rejection.

- Those with power are always tempted to use the law to preserve their own comfort. I pray for the integrity of all those in decision-making positions and for the courage of those who resist wrongdoing. I think of what I may need to do to stand for justice.

april 6–12

Something to think and pray about each day this week:

The Living God

The scholar John L. McKenzie, S.J., describes how the roots of Christian (and Jewish and Muslim) faith grew in "the desert wastes of Syria and Arabia, which seem to stretch into infinity." The Chosen People were in those wastes for forty years. Jesus himself recapitulated that experience of his people, by going into the wilderness for forty days. And Christians, following him, starting out on the forty days of Lent each year enter that desert experience too. But, in truth, our own day-to-day mundane lives often have something of that desert reality about them.

What happens out there, in the real, or in the man-made, deserts of today? Between the desert floor and the desert sky, life is stripped of all its artificial props, brought down to its essentials, in the effort to remain alive and avoid death. Vulnerable and exposed in that setting, we might also feel particularly threatened or tempted, as if surrounded by malignant forces in the swirling windswept sands. Such was the actual desert experience. But, more than this and above all, it was the place where the Chosen People experienced God: at Mount Sinai they were drawn into a covenant relationship. They could never forget that. In the desert—our illusions taken away, leaving us exposed and vulnerable—we find not nothingness, but the living God. God before us, God with us, the God of fidelity, and truth, and love.

The Presence of God

I reflect for a moment on God's presence
around me and in me.
Creator of the universe, the sun and the moon,
the earth,
every molecule, every atom, everything that is:
God is in every beat of my heart. God is with
me, now.

Freedom

A thick and shapeless tree-trunk would never
believe that it could become a statue, admired as
a miracle of sculpture, and would never submit
itself to the chisel of the sculptor, who sees by
her genius what she can make of it (St. Ignatius).
I ask for the grace to let myself be shaped by
my loving Creator.

Consciousness

Knowing that God loves me unconditionally,
I look honestly over the last day, its events and
my feelings.
Do I have something to be grateful for? Then,
I give thanks.
Is there something I am sorry for? Then, I ask
forgiveness.

The Word

I read the Word of God slowly, a few times
over, and I listen to what God is saying to me.
(Please turn to your scripture on the following
pages. Inspiration points are there should you
need them. When you are ready, return here to
continue.)

Conversation

What is stirring in me as I pray?
Am I consoled, troubled, left cold?

I imagine Jesus himself standing or sitting at
my side,
and share my feelings with him.

Conclusion

Glory be to the Father, and to the Son, and to
the Holy Spirit,
As it was in the beginning, is now and ever
shall be,
World without end. Amen.

Sunday 6th April,
Fifth Sunday of Lent   John 11:41–45

Jesus looked upwards and said, "Father, I thank you for having heard me. I knew that you always hear me, but I have said this for the sake of the crowd standing here, so that they may believe that you sent me." When he had said this, he cried with a loud voice, "Lazarus, come out!" The dead man came out, his hands and feet bound with strips of cloth, and his face wrapped in a cloth. Jesus said to them, "Unbind him, and let him go." Many of the Jews therefore, who had come with Mary and had seen what Jesus did, believed in him.

- Prayer brings us in touch with the body of Christ, of Jesus risen from death, and of Jesus present in all his people. Prayer affects the lives of others; in that way it is political, affecting how we live together, asking to be unbound and live in freedom like Lazarus.

- Knowing that others pray with *Sacred Space* can help my life of prayer.

Monday 7th April   John 8:7–11

When they kept on questioning Jesus, he straightened up and said to them, "Let anyone among you who is without sin be the first to throw a stone at her." And once again he bent down and wrote on the ground. When they heard it, they went away, one by one, beginning with the elders; and Jesus was left alone with the woman standing before him. Jesus straightened up and said to her, "Woman, where are they? Has no one condemned you?" She said, "No one, sir." And Jesus said, "Neither do I condemn you. Go your way, and from now on do not sin again."

- This story often invites people to heap criticism on the Pharisees; we can become critical, judgmental, and superior just as we notice these traits in the Pharisees. "Don't look out," Jesus says, "look in." I look in to my heart and become aware of my own need for forgiveness.

- What Jesus said to the woman he says to me, "I don't condemn you. Go on your way and don't sin." I am before Jesus—not condemned but being sent on my way—loved and trusted.

- If Jesus were to write a quiet message on the ground for me, what would it be?

Tuesday 8th April   John 8:21–30

Again Jesus said to them, "I am going away, and you will search for me, but you will die in your sin. Where I am going, you cannot come." Then the Jews said, "Is he going to kill himself? Is that what he means by saying, 'Where I am going, you cannot come'?" He said to them, "You are from below, I am from above; you are of this world, I am not of this world. I told you that you would die in your sins, for you will die in your sins unless you believe that I am he." They said to him, "Who are you?" Jesus said to them, "Why do I speak to you at all? I have much to say about you and much to condemn; but the one who sent me is true, and I declare to the world what I have heard from him." They did not understand that he was speaking to them about the Father. Jesus said to them, "When you have lifted up the Son of Man, then you will realize that I am he, and that I do nothing on my own, but I speak these things as the Father instructed me. And the one who sent me is with me; he has not left me alone, for I always do what is pleasing to him." As he was saying these things, many believed in him.

- The people who heard Jesus' message often took in just the words on the surface. His meaning was hidden from them when they failed to listen on a deeper level, to reflect about what his words might mean for them.

- This is the work of our prayer: to receive the Word of God into our hearts, to go beyond superficial—even important—meanings.

Wednesday 9th April   John 8:31–42

Then Jesus said to the Jews who had believed in him, "If you continue in my word, you are truly my disciples; and you will know the truth, and the truth will make you free." They answered him, "We are descendants of Abraham and have never been slaves to anyone. What do you mean by saying, 'You will be made free'?" Jesus answered them, "Very truly, I tell you, everyone who commits sin is a slave to sin. The slave does not have a permanent place in the household; the son has a place there forever. So if the Son makes you free, you will be free indeed. I know that you are descendants of Abraham; yet you look for an opportunity to kill me, because there is no place in you for my word. I declare what I have seen in the Father's presence; as for you, you should do what you have heard from the Father." They answered him, "Abraham is our father." Jesus said to them, "If you were Abraham's children, you would be doing what Abraham did, but now you are trying to kill me, a man who has told you the truth that I heard from God. This is not what Abraham did. You are indeed doing what your father does." They said to him, "We are not illegitimate children; we have one father, God himself." Jesus said to them, "If God were your Father, you would love me, for I came from God and now I am here. I did not come on my own, but he sent me."

- Jesus wants to lead me into truth so that I may be free. If I truly desire freedom, I need to be ready to accept the truth. There is nothing threatening

or accusatory here—it is about being known fully
and loved deeply.

- John shows the people who listened to Jesus
as being prickly and precious, quick to defend
their religion and righteousness. Jesus' replies
show them that they have forgotten love and
relationship.

Thursday 10th April   John 8:51–56

Jesus said, "Very truly, I tell you, whoever
keeps my word will never see death." The
Jews said to him, "Now we know that you have
a demon. Abraham died, and so did the prophets; yet you say, 'Whoever keeps my word will
never taste death.' Are you greater than our
father Abraham, who died? The prophets also
died. Who do you claim to be?" Jesus answered,
"If I glorify myself, my glory is nothing. It is my
Father who glorifies me, he of whom you say,
'He is our God,' though you do not know him.

But I know him; if I were to say that I do not know him, I would be a liar like you. But I do know him and I keep his word. Your ancestor Abraham rejoiced that he would see my day; he saw it and was glad."

- Lent helps me to recover my sincerity, to restoring my relationship with God. Jesus calls me to conversion, to leave aside any images or notions to which I have become attached.

- Jesus promises me life if I keep his word. What is his word for me today?

Friday 11th April   John 10:31–38

The Jews took up stones again to stone him. Jesus replied, "I have shown you many good works from the Father. For which of these are you going to stone me?" The Jews answered, "It is not for a good work that we are going to stone you, but for blasphemy, because you, though only a human being, are making yourself

God." Jesus answered, "Is it not written in your law, 'I said, you are gods'? If those to whom the word of God came were called 'gods'—and the scripture cannot be annulled—can you say that the one whom the Father has sanctified and sent into the world is blaspheming because I said, 'I am God's Son'? If I am not doing the works of my Father, then do not believe me. But if I do them, even though you do not believe me, believe the works, so that you may know and understand that the Father is in me and I am in the Father."

- The message of Jesus was threatening to the people of his time and remains threatening today. What might have to change for me if I were to accept what Jesus proclaims?

- Jesus asserts the dignity that I have in being a child of God. I pray for people who suffer injustice.

- I think of what I might do to express the vision that Jesus gives me.

Saturday 12th April   **John 11:45–48**

Many of the Jews therefore, who had come with Mary and had seen what Jesus did, believed in him. But some of them went to the Pharisees and told them what he had done. So the chief priests and the Pharisees called a meeting of the council, and said, "What are we to do? This man is performing many signs. If we let him go on like this, everyone will believe in him, and the Romans will come and destroy both our holy place and our nation."

- The leaders saw that believing in Jesus would threaten much of the security that they knew. It may be so with me; I might have to correct comfortable habits or give up patterns that I have settled into.

- It is not possible to believe in Jesus and to let life be unchanged. I acknowledge that my way of living shows signs of following Jesus and ask for the strength and courage I need to be a calm and confident disciple.

Something to think and pray about each day this week:

Staying the Journey

In this Holy Week, now upon us, we see Jesus entering the dark realm of his suffering and death. The whole course of his earthly life has led to this—to the brief applause and "hosannas" when entering Jerusalem, to the Passover Supper with his disciples, to the agony of Gethsemane, the betrayal and arrest, followed by his condemnation by the religious and civil authorities, and his being done to death by crucifixion outside the city walls. We, however, try to stay with him these days—even though that staying seemed impossible for his disciples then: "All of them deserted him and fled" (Mk 14:50). Only the women, including his mother, and the beloved disciple, stood by him (Jn 19:25). All his life, surely, from his infancy by Mary's side, was moving towards this place. And dimly we can see, in it all, the momentum of a great unending love, by which "God so loved the world that he gave his only Son" (Jn 3:16). So we look towards him, and at that love. We look too at the faces of people stricken by natural disaster, death, and war. And all of us, in turn, are looked upon by the Father, and through the eyes of the beloved Son . . . this is God's way . . . in vulnerable brokenness, into our hearts, and drawing us into eternal life. This is God's deepest meaning.

The Presence of God

In the silence of my innermost being,
in the fragments of my yearned-for wholeness,
can I hear the whispers of God's presence?
Can I remember when I felt God's nearness?

When we walked together and I let myself be embraced by God's love?

Freedom

There are very few people who realize what God would make of them if they abandoned themselves into his hands, and let themselves be formed by his grace (St. Ignatius).
I ask for the grace to trust myself totally to God's love.

Consciousness

How do I find myself today?
Where am I with God? With others?
Do I have something to be grateful for? Then I give thanks.
Is there something I am sorry for? Then I ask forgiveness.

The Word

I take my time to read the Word of God, slowly, a few times, allowing myself to dwell on anything that strikes me. (Please turn to your scripture on the following pages. Inspiration points are there should you need them. When you are ready, return here to continue.)

Conversation

Do I notice myself reacting as I pray with the Word of God?
Do I feel challenged, comforted, angry?
Imagining Jesus sitting or standing by me,
I speak out my feelings, as one trusted friend to another.

Conclusion

Glory be to the Father, and to the Son, and to the Holy Spirit,
As it was in the beginning, is now and ever shall be,
World without end. Amen.

Sunday 13th April, Palm Sunday
of the Lord's Passion   Matthew 21:1–9

When they had come near Jerusalem and had reached Bethphage, at the Mount of Olives, Jesus sent two disciples, saying to them, "Go into the village ahead of you, and immediately you will find a donkey tied, and a colt with her; untie them and bring them to me. If anyone says anything to you, just say this, 'The Lord needs them.' And he will send them immediately." This took place to fulfill what had been spoken through the prophet, saying, "Tell the daughter of Zion, Look, your king is coming to you, humble, and mounted on a donkey, and on a colt, the foal of a donkey." The disciples went and did as Jesus had directed them; they brought the donkey and the colt, and put their cloaks on them, and he sat on them. A very large crowd spread their cloaks on the road, and others cut branches from the trees and spread them on the road. The crowds that went ahead of him and that followed were shouting, "Hosanna to the Son of David! Blessed is the one who comes in the name of the Lord! Hosanna in the highest heaven!"

- Christ's death is like a bridge; he lay on the cross and was crucified, forming the bridge between nations and also between ourselves. Jesus can be the bridge between us all because he knows everything human—even to death. He fulfills all these conditions!

- Holy Week is "The week of the bridge." That makes it holy. Any week we build bridges among people is holy week.

Monday 14th April   John 12:1–6

Six days before the Passover, Jesus came to Bethany, the home of Lazarus, whom he had raised from the dead. There they gave a dinner for him. Martha served, and Lazarus was one of those at the table with him. Mary took a pound of costly perfume made of pure nard, anointed Jesus' feet, and wiped them with her hair. The house was filled with the fragrance of the perfume. But Judas Iscariot, one of his disciples (the one who was about to betray him), said, "Why was this perfume not sold for three hundred denarii and the money given to the poor?" (He said this not because he cared about the poor, but because he was a thief; he kept the common purse and used to steal what was put into it.)

- Breathe deeply in and imagine the smell of a precious scent filling the house. It was an extravagant, wasteful, and indulgent thing to do, but it spoke of a human reality: some opportunities need to be grasped as they arise, some moments need to be honoured, friendship cannot always be calculating.

- Holy Week invites me to spend time with Jesus, not for any logical reason, but simply to accompany a loved friend.

Tuesday 15th April   John 13:31–33, 36–38

When Judas had gone out, Jesus said, "Now the Son of Man has been glorified, and God has been glorified in him. If God has been glorified in him, God will also glorify him in himself and will glorify him at once. Little children, I am with you only a little longer. You will look for me; and as I said to the Jews so now I say to you, 'Where I am going, you cannot come.'" Simon Peter said to him, "Lord, where are you going?" Jesus answered, "Where I am going, you cannot follow me now; but you will follow afterwards." Peter said to him, "Lord, why can I not follow you now? I will lay down my life for you." Jesus answered, "Will you lay down your life for me? Very truly, I tell you, before the cock crows, you will have denied me three times."

- Following Jesus requires recognizing how he chooses, where he goes, what he might do or say.

I take time during these days to consider deeply what is in Jesus' heart and how, even when he is in turmoil, his thoughts are for his friends.

- Peter's best intentions were not matched by his performance. I know what that is like. I allow myself to be forgiven by God and to be trusted still to act in Jesus' name.

Wednesday 16th April
Matthew 26:14–16, 20–25

Then one of the twelve, who was called Judas Iscariot, went to the chief priests and said, "What will you give me if I betray him to you?" They paid him thirty pieces of silver. And from that moment he began to look for an opportunity to betray him. When it was evening, Jesus took his place with the twelve; and while they were eating, he said, "Truly I tell you, one of you will betray me." And they became greatly distressed and began to say to him one after another, "Surely not I, Lord?" He answered, "The one who has dipped his hand into the bowl with me will betray me. The Son of Man goes as it is written of him, but woe to that one by whom the Son of Man is betrayed! It would have been better for that one not to have been born." Judas, who betrayed him, said, "Surely not I, Rabbi?" He replied, "You have said so."

- Thirty pieces of silver was a high price; Jesus has often been betrayed for less. The deal does not always involve money; the currencies of comfort, popularity, influence, and power are often acceptable forms of payment.

- Although he saw that he might be betrayed, Jesus did not turn from the disciples or from giving himself to them. He did not let their distress silence him, but he spoke the truth to them, knowing it would be unwelcome.

Thursday 17th April, Holy Thursday

John 13:2–15

During supper, Jesus, knowing that the Father had given all things into his hands, and that he had come from God and was going to God, got up from the table, took off his outer robe, and tied a towel around himself. Then he poured water into a basin and began to wash the disciples' feet and to wipe them with the towel that was tied around him. He came to Simon Peter, who said to him, "Lord, are you going to wash my feet?" Jesus answered, "You do not know now what I am doing, but later you will understand." Peter said to him, "You will never wash my feet." Jesus answered, "Unless I wash you, you have no share with me." Simon Peter said to him, "Lord, not my feet only but also my hands and my head!" Jesus said to him, "One who has bathed does not need to wash, except for the feet, but is entirely clean. And you are clean, though not all of you." For he knew who was to betray him; for this reason he said, "Not all of you are clean." After Jesus had washed their feet, had put on his robe, and had returned to the table, he said to them, "Do you know what I have done to you? You call me Teacher and Lord—and you are right, for that is what I am. So if I, your Lord and Teacher, have washed your feet, you also ought to wash one another's feet. For I have set you an example, that you also should do as I have done to you."

- John the Evangelist communicates to us what is at the heart of the Eucharist, not by describing the action with bread and wine, but by giving us a lingering look at the servant heart of Jesus.

- I humbly give thanks for my opportunities to be of service to others. I pray that even my small acts of service may be for the good of the world and for the glory of God.

Friday 18th April,
Good Friday John 18:1–5

After Jesus had spoken these words, he went out with his disciples across the Kidron valley to a place where there was a garden, which he and his disciples entered. Now Judas, who betrayed him, also knew the place, because Jesus often met there with his disciples. So Judas brought a detachment of soldiers together with police from the chief priests and the Pharisees, and they came there with lanterns and torches and weapons. Then Jesus, knowing all that was to happen to him, came forward and asked them, "For whom are you looking?" They answered, "Jesus of Nazareth." Jesus replied, "I am he." Judas, who betrayed him, was standing with them.

- The betrayal of Jesus happened in a garden, reminding us of the earlier rejection of God's ways in the Garden of Eden. God can be forgotten even when we are surrounded by natural goodness.

- When I see a cross or crucifix I think, "for me," as I recall Jesus' love for me. I think of how I might create some space this day to remember Jesus' going to the cross. I ask for the help I need as I take up the crosses that I find in my life.

Saturday 19th April,
Holy Saturday   Matthew 27:57–66

When it was evening, there came a rich man from Arimathea, named Joseph, who was also a disciple of Jesus. He went to Pilate and asked for the body of Jesus; then Pilate ordered it to be given to him. So Joseph took the body and wrapped it in a clean linen cloth and laid it in his own new tomb, which he had hewn in the rock. He then rolled a great stone to the door of the tomb and went away. Mary Magdalene and the other Mary were there, sitting opposite the tomb. The next day, that is, after the day of Preparation, the chief priests and the Pharisees gathered before Pilate and said, "Sir, we remember what that impostor said while he was still alive, 'After three days I will rise again.' Therefore command that the tomb be made secure until the third day; otherwise his disciples may go and steal him away, and tell the people, 'He has been raised from the dead,' and the last deception would be worse than the first." Pilate said to them, "You have a guard of soldiers; go, make it as secure as you can." So they went with the guard and made the tomb secure by sealing the stone.

- This quiet day of waiting at the tomb draws me into a compassion for all who are waiting, uncertain, or who hold on to fragile hope.

- I think of those who await medical results, of people in prison, of those whose dreams have been crushed.

- I wait for the Lord, drawing strength from the company of others and from the memory of God's goodness, in hope of more of God's goodness in the future.

april 20

Something to think and pray about each day this week:

Into the New Light

Can light come from deepest darkness? Many women cry out from their desolation on behalf of "the disappeared"—their husbands and their children—who have been violently taken away to be no more. "Death and the hells of dereliction and abandonment eat up men and women, exhaust them, scrape them out and bring them to nothing" (Rowan Williams, *Open to Judgement*). But on this Easter day, the women who have waited in that most dreadful darkness have found a light dawning. It was "still dark" (Jn 20:1), indeed, when Mary of Magdala came to the tomb, where the body of Jesus had been laid.

Next, the beloved disciple, who had been with the women by the cross, came to a dawning of faith as he looked into the empty tomb: "He saw, and he believed," even though he saw no person. And then Mary, in the beautiful garden scene, finds herself called by name, "Mary!"— and there is Jesus, before her, alive, risen, the One for whom her heart yearned. And all is changed, utterly. For us, too, that transforming Easter faith is offered to us. And that dawning faith can change everything.

The Presence of God
God is with me, but more,
God is within me, giving me existence.
Let me dwell for a moment on God's life-giving presence
in my body, my mind, my heart
and in the whole of my life.

Freedom

Many countries are at this moment suffering
the agonies of war.
I bow my head in thanksgiving for my
freedom.
I pray for all prisoners and captives.

Consciousness

I remind myself that I am in the presence of
the Lord.
I will take refuge in his loving heart.
He is my strength in times of weakness.
He is my comforter in times of sorrow.

The Word

I read the Word of God slowly, a few times
over, and I listen to what God is saying to me.
(Please turn to your scripture on the following
pages. Inspiration points are there should you
need them. When you are ready, return here to
continue.)

Conversation

How has God's Word moved me? Has it left
me cold?

Has it consoled me or moved me to act in a
new way?

I imagine Jesus standing or sitting beside me,
I turn and share my feelings with him.

Conclusion

Glory be to the Father, and to the Son, and to
the Holy Spirit,

As it was in the beginning, is now and ever
shall be,

World without end. Amen.

Sunday 20th April,
Easter Sunday   John 20:1–9

Early on the first day of the week, while it was still dark, Mary Magdalene came to the tomb and saw that the stone had been removed from the tomb. So she ran and went to Simon Peter and the other disciple, the one whom Jesus loved, and said to them, "They have taken the Lord out of the tomb, and we do not know where they have laid him." Then Peter and the other disciple set out and went toward the tomb. The two were running together, but the other disciple outran Peter and reached the tomb first. He bent down to look in and saw the linen wrappings lying there, but he did not go in. Then Simon Peter came, following him, and went into the tomb. He saw the linen wrappings lying there, and the cloth that had been on Jesus' head, not lying with the linen wrappings but rolled up in a place by itself. Then the other disciple, who reached the tomb first, also went in, and he saw and believed; for as yet they did not understand the scripture, that he must rise from the dead.

- When Jesus raised Lazarus, Lazarus had to be freed from his grave-clothes. Jesus' grave-clothes are rolled up and lying on the side, a reflection of his mastery over death.

- I stand in the doorway beside the entrance and stare into that empty tomb. Do I grasp the difference between this resurrection and that of Lazarus?

The Irish Jesuits are engaged in a wide range of ministries both at home and throughout the world. They serve as teachers, caregivers for homeless youth, parish priests, academics, artists, and administrators. Their website, sacredspace.ie, attracts more than six million visits annually and is produced in some twenty languages.

Founded in 1865, Ave Maria Press,
a ministry of the Congregation of
Holy Cross, is a Catholic publishing
company that serves the spiritual and
formative needs of the Church and its
schools, institutions, and ministers;
Christian individuals and families; and
others seeking spiritual nourishment.

For a complete listing of titles from

Ave Maria Press

Sorin Books

Forest of Peace

Christian Classics

visit www.avemariapress.com

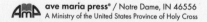 ave maria press® / Notre Dame, IN 46556
A Ministry of the United States Province of Holy Cross